How to Meditate
on God's Word

DANIEL C. OKPARA

Fast and Easy Ways to Practice Intentional Bible Meditation and Grow in Faith, Worship and Prayer

Published By:

Better Life Media.

BETTER LIFE WORLD OUTREACH CENTER.

Website: www.BetterLifeWorld.org

Email: info@betterlifeworld.org

This title and others are available for quantity discounts for sale promotions, gifts, and evangelism. Visit our website or email us to get started.

Any scripture quotation in this book is taken from the King James Version or New International Version, except where stated. Used by permission.

All texts, calls, letters, testimonies, and inquiries are welcome.

CONTENTS

FREE BONUS ...

Download These 4 Powerful Books Today for
FREE... And Take Your Relationship With God
to a New Level.

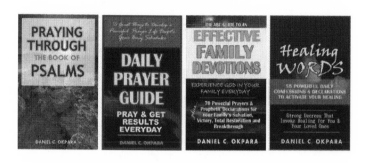

Go Here to Download:

www.betterlifeworld.org/grow

INTRODUCTION

"This book of the law shall not depart out of thy mouth; but thou shalt meditate therein day and night, that thou mayest observe to do according to all that is written therein: for then thou shalt make thy way prosperous, and then thou shalt have good success." -

Joshua 1:8

It was time for Moses to leave the scene. He had fought a good fight, but he would not be leading the Israelites to the Promised Land. Someone else must fill his position.

God chose the man, Joshua, to take his

place. He was given a series of instructions that would ensure he succeeded. One of those instructions is what we read above.

In simple terms, God was telling Joshua to:

- Read the book of the law

- Meditate on what you read

- Continue to declare it

If he did those three things, he would be able to remember and do what the Book says, and consequently, he would be prosperous and have great success.

Those are the same things God is saying to us today. If we desire to prosper and have good success, then we must...

- Read the book of the Law (the Word of God)

- Meditate on what we read

- Continue to declare the Word

This three-step instruction is the formula for daily victory and breakthrough in life.

Meditation plays a vital role in our relationship with God. As the Bible says, it helps us to discover and obey what the Lord is speaking to us, and lead us to success.

A lot of people read the Bible just as though they were reading a novel. However, to understand the message God is passing across through the Bible, you need to meditate on it. Meditation is what will give you insight into God's plan for you and empower your obedience.

Unfortunately, meditation is not easy; it does not come easy for most of us, because of the distractions we continually face: world news, breaking news, social media and propaganda, political issues, family matters and so on. Never have we faced the kind of distractions that we face now! It's hard to find anyone who's not busy with so many things today.

However, if you desire to learn more of God's ways, hear His voice, and grow in your spiritual life, then you need to practice more meditation in your life.

This book contains practical, but easy,

guidelines to meditate on God's word and hear His voice as you do. I am double sure that these meditation ideas will change your life for good.

Chapter 1: What is Meditation?

"O how love I thy law! it is my meditation all the day. Thou through thy commandments hast made me wiser than mine enemies: for they are ever with me."

- Psalm 119:97-98

Bible meditation is not the mystical or existentialistic efforts designed to connect one to spiritual quietness. Meditating on the Word of God is totally different from that which most people associate with meditation.

In Hebrew, the word meditate is

"hagah." It means "to utter, to devise, to muse," "to mutter."

The key here is *to utter focus scriptures over and over again and muse over them.* The word muse means **"to consider something thoughtfully and thoroughly."**

That is exactly what Bible meditation should be - *to mutter scriptures with our mouths, speak it in our minds, over and over again, and to consider it thoughtfully and thoroughly.*

While most meditations taught today simply refer to the quietness of the mind, Biblical meditation gives us the object of meditation: **The WORDS of God.** *It involves purging the mind of things that are wrong and filling it with* *things as inspired by the scriptures.*

In simple terms, Biblical meditation means to read the Bible, mutter the verses read to oneself repeatedly, and then spend some time thinking or pondering on what you have read.

Meditation is the way to develop your spirit man. It helps get our minds better prepared for prayer. We are better able to focus and worship God in spirit and in truth.

As you meditate on God's word, you help your spirit, soul, and body become more detached from the influences of the world; you detach your affections from what's not necessary and re-channel them to the most important things of life. You open yourself up to divine encounters that will establish your destiny.

The Bible says:

Guard your heart above all else, for it determines the course of your life. - Proverbs 4:23 (NLV)

By practicing meditation, we're able to protect our hearts which determines the course of our lives; we're able to yield more to the LORD and discern His leadings. And as the Psalmist said, *we become wiser than our enemies.*

Why Should We Meditate?

The book of Proverbs 4:20-22 says, *"My son, pay attention to my words and be willing to learn; Open your ears to my sayings. Do not let them escape from your sight; Keep them in the center of your heart; for they are life to those who find them, and healing and health to all their flesh"* (AMP).

Notice from those verses that when you "pay attention" to God's words, they become "His sayings." That is, God begins to talk to you through them. The Holy Spirit amplifies the Words inside of you and gives you details that could have only come from God. You gain direction.

That's why we meditate.

The Psalmist gives us at least five reasons for meditating on God's Word. They are:

1. To focus: *I will meditate on your precepts and fix my eyes on your ways* (Psalm 119:15 - ESV)

As we read our Bibles over lunch, or in bed, we face a lot of distractions. But when we close our eyes and start meditating on the Words we read, we shut ourselves out of those distractions and fix our eyes on Christ – even if it's just for a few minutes. Over time, this practice helps us to improve our concentration.

2. To understand: *Make me understand the way of Your precepts, So that I will meditate (focus my thoughts) on Your wonderful works* (Psalm 119:27 - AMP)

When we meditate, we seek to

comprehend the wonderful works of God in the universe. As we pray like the Psalmist, "Make me understand your teachings, LORD," the Holy Spirit begins to give us insights and revelations about God's ways that builds our faith and strengthens our relationship with Him.

3. To remember: *I remember the days of old; I meditate on all that You have done; I ponder the work of Your hands.* (Psalm 143:5 – AMP)

Meditation helps us to cast our minds back and recollect the great stories of the Bible, the plan of salvation and the gift of the Holy Spirit. Through meditation, we are able to remember the works of God in our lives in the past and draw closer to Him in worship.

4. For devotion: *Oh, how I love Your law! It is my meditation all the day.* (Psalm 119:97 - AMP)

The primary focus of meditation is worship.

Our hearts often don't delight in God's Word. We are tempted to stop reading, to lose focus, to move on to other things. But meditation "captures" our hearts to delight in God's Word, and draw us to worship.

5. To Act on the Word: As Joshua 1:8 says, it is through meditation that we are able to hear and understand what the LORD is asking us to do. Then we're able to muster the courage and faith to obey Him, despite the situation of things.

Types of Meditation

---

1. Casual Meditation

Just as the Bible has admonished us to pray without ceasing, we can as also meditate without ceasing.

It means that we can meditate while in the car, in the office, on the plane, during launch or office break. We can pull up a particular verse in our minds or skim one or two scriptures and begin to think on them.

That way, we're staying our minds on God.

Somehow, the Holy Spirit will still quicken in us powerful insights for our victory and worship.

2. Intentional Meditation

Study to shew thyself approved unto God, a workman that needeth not to be ashamed, rightly dividing the word of truth - 2 Timothy 2:15

In intentional meditation, you deliberately take out time to go somewhere and meditate. It doesn't have to be some distant place. It could be beside your bed, sitting room, or any other place. The difference is that you're deliberating taking time out to be with God. It could be while others have gone to bed, or you wake up in the middle of the night to be alone, to read the Bible, to meditate and to pray.

Jesus practiced intentional meditation often. He would often leave the house and go somewhere to meditate and pray.

The Bible says, *"Very early in the morning, while it was still dark, Jesus got up, left the house and went off to a solitary place, where he prayed."* (Mark 1:35 – NIV, See also Matthew 14:13, 23, Luke 4:42-43, 5:16, Mark 6:42-48).

That's the model for us who wish to grow in the knowledge of God and bear fruit for the kingdom. As much as we can, we must take some time out, stay awake, free from any distraction, to read the Bible, meditate and pray.

Both types of meditation are necessary. We'll need to maximize every moment we can to draw closer to God as we go about our daily businesses as believers.

Chapter 2: 10 Benefits of Meditating on God's Word

"Let the words of my mouth, and the meditation of my heart, be acceptable in thy sight, O LORD, my strength, and my redeemer." - Psalms 19:14

The benefits we get from meditating on scriptures are many, but here are a few to challenge you, to inspire you to practice more meditation in your life.

1. Meditation grows your faith

Several nights ago, I was meditating on Luke 10:18-20. Before this time, we faced a situation where some evil-minded people were coming to plant charms in the property site we were developing. As I thought about those verses, the Holy Spirit gave me another connecting scripture: Psalm 125:3, which says,

---

"For the rod of the wicked shall not rest upon the lot of the righteous; lest the righteous put forth their hands unto iniquity."

The *"lot of the righteous"* as rendered in other versions says, *"the land allotted to the righteous."*

Rod in the Bible usually talks about *"power, strength, decrees, etc."* In essence, God is saying that the power, decrees and charms of the wicked ones will not have any effect on the land (property) of the righteous. As long as we had legal authority (through purchase or inheritance) over that land, nothing they do would have any effect.

Those insights inspired a lion faith in me, and I knew that they were wasting their time.

When we meditate on God's Words, we connect with supernatural insights that embolden our faith and give us victory in our day-to-day situations and experiences.

2. Meditation strengthens our prayer life

As we meditate and gain supernatural

insights, the Holy Spirit inspires us to a prayer life not made up of our conventional designs.

For example, as I saw those scriptures, I arose in a holy anger and made some heaven-backed decrees over that property.

There have been times, during meditation, that I would begin to pray for someone, for a church, for a nation, or for friends, that I didn't have in mind earlier on to pray for. The Holy Spirit would quicken my heart for those prayers. That's what meditation does.

Meditation will strengthen your prayer life beyond your wildest imagination. You'll find yourself praying in ways, and for things, you wouldn't have thought about. In the long run, your prayer life and experiences will be better for it.

3. Keeps the Word within our hearts

My son, pay attention to my words and be willing to learn; Open your ears to my sayings. Do not let them escape from your sight; Keep them in the center of your heart. For they are life to those who find them, and healing and health to all their flesh - Proverbs 4:20-22 (AMP)

How else would we be able to keep the Words of God in the center of our hearts if not through intentional meditation?

4. Meditation renews our minds

Don't copy the behavior and customs of this world, but let God transform you into a new person by changing the way you think. Then you will learn to know God's will for you, which is good and pleasing and perfect. – Rom. 12:2 (NLV)

Life is all about the way we think. It's our responsibility to take the Words of God and think on what they are saying. As we do that in humility, God transforms us; we are better able to discern His will and follow His plans, not the traditions of men.

There are many customs and traditions that we are unknowingly allowing to decide how we live. We may never know how these traditions are limiting our lives until we get the Words of God into our hearts and begin to think on them. Then it starts to divide our souls and spirits and show us the difference (Hebrews 4:12).

Apostle Paul says in Philippians 4: 8 that we should think about things that are true, honest, just, pure, of good reports, virtue, and praise. What else is truer than the Word of God?

5. Meditation keeps your heart at peace

Thou wilt keep him in perfect peace, whose mind is stayed on thee: because he trusteth in thee - Isaiah 26:3.

As we meditate on scriptures, we gain insights that embolden our faith, stir our prayer life, and assure our hearts that God is in control. Then the peace of God that passes all understanding rests in our spirits, despite how things may appear physically

6. Empowers us to walk away from sin

Thy word have I hid in mine heart, that I might not sin against thee. - Psalm 119:11

The Psalmist is saying that it's not possible for us to avoid the myriad of temptations that we face daily if the Word of God is not deeply planted in our hearts. Opportunities to sin and disobey God will always present themselves to us. At such times, the Words of God in our hearts will be quickened by the Holy Spirit, and suddenly, we'll know what to do; and not just know what to do, we'll be able to muster the courage to do what God wants us to do.

Blessed is the man that walketh not in the counsel of the ungodly, nor standeth in the way of sinners, nor sitteth in the seat of the scornful.

But his delight is in the law of the LORD; and in his law doth he meditate day and night.

And he shall be like a tree planted by the rivers of water, that bringeth forth his fruit in his season; his leaf also shall not wither; and whatsoever he doeth shall prosper - Psalm 1:1-3

7. Empowers our worship

My soul shall be satisfied as with marrow and fatness; and my mouth shall praise thee with joyful lips: When I remember thee upon my bed, and meditate on thee in the night watches. -

Psalm 63:5-6

As we ponder and remember the fathomlessness of God, our hearts are drawn to worship and reverence. We are forced to sing out or declare His greatness. We are filled with awe of His love and our underserving of it. And we recommit to serving Him in humility.

That's what the Bible refers to as worshipping God in truth and in spirit.

I will meditate in thy precepts, and have respect unto thy ways - Psalm 119:15

8. God speaks to us in meditation

This Book of the Law shall not depart from your mouth, but you shall read [and meditate on] it day and night, so that you may be careful to do [everything] in accordance with all that is written in it; for then you will make your way prosperous, and then you will be successful - **Joshua 1:8 (AMP)**

My son, pay attention to my words and be willing to learn; Open your ears to my sayings. Do not let them escape from your sight; Keep them in the center of your heart. For they are life to those who find them, and healing and health to all their flesh – Prov. 4:20-22 (AMP).

God speaks to us during meditation. Somehow, we learn what we should do and how to respond to certain issues we may be faced with.

9. Meditation connects us to supernatural wisdom

My mouth shall speak of wisdom, and the meditation of my heart shall be of understanding. - Psalms 49:3

10. Meditation helps our retentive memory

Meditation requires that we spend time on God's word, repeatedly say the verses we are meditating on, and try to ponder them. In the long run, this practice helps to improve our memory.

Chapter 3: The 7-Step Method for Effective Meditation

"When you "pay attention" to God's words, they become "His sayings." That is, God begins to talk to you through them. The Holy Spirit amplifies the Words inside of you and gives you details that could have only come from God. You gain direction."

Okay, let's get down to the practice of meditation. The following seven-step process will help you get the best out of your Bible meditation times.

1. Choose the Scripture

The Bible is comprised of 66 books,

divided into hundreds of chapters and verses. The first thing to do anytime you want to meditate on it is to choose exactly what you want to mediate on. Are you going to meditate on:

- A verse or couple of verses

- A story

- A chapter

- A subject (a particular theme)

Once you decide that this is the scripture (a verse, a chapter, a story or a subject area) you'll be meditating, then you can proceed to the next step.

Let's take an example of two verses for clarification as we read along. Let's use 2 Corinthians 1:3-4.

2. Read It

Before you embark on meditating a scripture, you need to read it first. It is recommended that you read the particular verse, story or chapter you want to meditate on more than once. I usually read it with more than one translation to get a general understanding of what that place is talking about.

Using our example meditation verses above, we will now read what they say.

Blessed be the God and Father of our Lord Jesus Christ, the Father of mercies and God of all comfort; who comforteth us in all our affliction, that we may be able to comfort them that are in any affliction, through the comfort wherewith we ourselves are comforted of God. (ASV)

Blessed be God, even the Father of our Lord Jesus Christ, the Father of mercies, and the God of all comfort;

Who comforteth us in all our tribulation, that we may be able to comfort them which are in any trouble, by the comfort wherewith we ourselves are comforted of God. (KJV)

Blessed [gratefully praised and adored] be the God and Father of our Lord Jesus Christ, the Father of mercies and the God of all comfort, 4 who comforts and encourages us in every trouble so that we will be able to comfort and encourage those who are in any kind of trouble, with the comfort with which we ourselves are comforted by God. –

(AMP)

There are three translations presented up there: The American Standard Version (ASV), the King James Version (KJV), and the Amplified Version (AMP).

As I said, the reason for reading more than one version is to have a general overview of what the particular scripture is talking about.

After reading, we are now ready to move on to the next step.

3. Recite It

Recite means to repeat the words, as from memory.

Once you've read a story, a verse, or a chapter that you want to meditate, close your eyes and begin to recite it. Don't worry; you're not expected to recite everything word for word. Just open your mouth and begin to repeat or re-tell that scripture to yourself.

This process is important in the meditation process, as it does two things to you. One, you understand it more. Two, your memory picks it and registers it onwards.

So taking our scripture focus, for example, I would begin to recite the Words...

Praise be to the Father of our LORD Jesus Christ, the Father of mercies. He comforts us in our troubles so that we will be able to comfort others in trouble with the comfort that He has comforted us.

As I said, it doesn't have to be exactly as the bible stated it word-for-word. Recite it in your own words if need be. The most important thing in Bible meditation is to grasp the message God is passing across.

And please note that to recite something, you have to say it with your mouth, not just in your mind. That's what the Bible means when it says *"This book of the law should not depart from your mouth"* (Joshua 1:8). It means that you should open your mouth and mumble it repeatedly to yourself, with the intention of understanding what it is saying.

4. Ponder it

As you recite the scripture, the next step is to ponder on it. To ponder is to think about something. You may say that this is the meditation time. Yes, you're right.

I usually ask myself a few questions, like:

- Who said this?
- Who was he talking to?
- Who was he talking about?
- What was he trying to teach them?

- What was he telling the recipients to do?

- Can I remember any connecting scripture to this one?

- How does this apply to me?

As you ask yourself these questions, you're now ready to move on to the next step.

5. Write It

As you ask yourself those questions, answers will flow in your mind; you'll get lots of inspiration. You should write these inspired thoughts on a notepad.

You may not write every detail, just write a few thoughts to remind yourself later about your takeaway from that meditation.

Taking our focus verses for example,

here are answers I get as I think about it.

- Paul wrote this

- He was talking to the believers at Corinth, which by extension is us (me)

- He was talking about God

- He was trying to tell them that God will not abandon them. That He would comfort them so that they can comfort others.

- God will not abandon me. He is a father of comfort. He will surely make a way for me.

- When God comforts me, He also wants me to comfort others going through similar things.

After you've scribbled down the thoughts that strike your heart as you think on the verse, or chapter, or story, then move on to the next step.

6. Pray it

Praying the scripture is also a part of the meditation process. It could be a prayer of worship, a prayer of declaration, a prayer for others, etc.

Taking our focus scripture, for example, I pray thus:

Father, I thank You because You are the Father of mercy.

You comfort us in our situations so that we will comfort others with the same comfort.

I am sure that You will always comfort me in all situations, providing me a way of escape - always.

Please Father, Always remind me by Your Spirit, as I'm comforted by you, to comfort others as well.

In Jesus name I pray.

Praying scripture is the most powerful way to pray in God's will. As you do pray the verse you have just meditated, you're ready to go to the next step.

7. Apply it

The scripture finds its power in the application; for faith without works is dead.

Meditation inspires your faith, action, and implementation produces the blessings.

So taking the sample scripture you've just meditated, the next thing would be to ask, "LORD, how do I apply this scripture?"

There must be a way to apply it, even if it's in small steps.

Here's the thing: Before God, there are no small steps, only faith steps. Every action inspired by faith in God's Word, no matter how little, produces great exploits.

Let's Recap.

Here are the seven simple ways to meditate on God's Word:

1. Chose the scripture
2. Read it
3. Recite it
4. Ponder Over it
5. Write it
6. Pray it
7. Apply it

As you do this from time to time, you'll

find that your understanding of God and His voice is growing continually; and you'll be productive for the kingdom of God and humanity.

I'll also advise that you start with easier to understand scriptures before moving on to the difficult ones. Also, some scripture-verses are already words of prayer; while you read them out, believe and claim them for yourself and your family.

Meditation is not a one-time thing. Do not assume that a few minutes of meditation on one occasion will bring you closer to God's Word for the rest of your life.

You need to consistently meditate, and work on it if you wish to accrue the benefits that comes from it. You have to learn to soak yourself in God's Word for the WORDS to be engraved in your heart.

Chapter 4: General Tips for Effective Bible Meditation

Here are a couple more general tips for effective Bible meditation.

1. You Need Tools for Bible Meditation

To be successful with meditation, you need a few tools to make the process smoother. Just as you need tools to mine gold from the earth, you also need tools to **extract truths** from the Bible.

- **You'll need a Bible dictionary:** These days, you can easily download a good Bible dictionary from the app stores. Take some time and do that. However, avoid being too theological. The essence of Bible meditation is to encounter God and not to win some Theological competition.

- **A Pen, Marker, and Notebook:** You need a marker, a pencil or pen, and a notebook so that you can mark places that strike your heart while reading, and take note of thoughts that well up from your spirit.

2. Choose a time and a place

If you want to go to the farm, you just don't go in the afternoon when the sun is at its highest point. Instead, it is always better to go in the morning while the sun is still waking up or in the evening when it is setting. This allows you ample time to work before the heat from the sun gets you tired and sweaty or before the darkness takes over.

This same principle works for

meditation.

If you are going to meditate successfully on God's word, you need to choose a period when you can meditate undisturbed and without any distractions, or distracting thoughts going on in your head. Early morning hours (12 AM – 7 AM) are usually the best times for intentional meditation. However, if the nature of your business does not allow this, you can meditate any time of the day. Whenever you can get to be alone with God is important.

If your bedroom, or sitting room, is quiet enough, then you can remain there and carry out your daily meditation. Where it is not, it is essential that you seek a place that would be quiet for you. A personal study room might be just the perfect place for you. Go with your Bible and other materials you may need and lock yourself in for the period you need to meditate.

One of the biggest distractions we have today is our phones. Avoid going in to your meditation points with your phone, unless you would need Bible dictionary apps in it to amplify your study. Where that is the case, it's fine to use your phone, but try as much as possible to avoid distractions coming from it.

3. Quiet your heart

We are humans, and there are lots of distracting thoughts we harbor in our minds. There are also difficulties we face that do not allow us to focus: The challenges of the day, the week or the past month, and so on. They sit in the mind and continue to trouble us all day. However, to successfully meditate on the Word, we need to surrender these thoughts to the Lord and focus only on the WORD. A good way to do this is by praying before we begin reading or trying to meditate. You can also sing some songs of praise and worship before going ahead with your meditation.

When you quiet your heart, you are assured of a great and fruitful time with God.

4. Choose an Easy to Understand Bible Translation

As I said earlier, meditation time is intended to grow your relationship with God, not to sound theologically correct. So choose a Bible translation that is easy to understand. I have personally found the Amplified Bible (AMP) and The Living Bible (TLB) very reader-friendly, without losing the Original message. If you have other versions you'd prefer, that's fine. And if you would rather stick with the King James Version (KJV), you're not also at fault. The point is to get a version that flows for you.

5. Choose a passage or a verse and read it over and over again

There are some hymns or poems you learned when you were younger that you can still easily recite today. Think about it. How did you learn this and carry them with you for so long? Simple. It's because you read and then recited these poems over and over again while you were young. They now stuck in your memory that you can easily remember them when the need arises.

As you prepare to meditate on the word of God, you need to choose a passage, a chapter, a story, or just a verse. Most times, it is better to thoroughly read the whole chapter or passage where the verse you want to meditate on can be found. This gives you a wider knowledge of that particular paragraph and helps you understand it better. You could just read the whole chapter once or twice, before focusing on the small passage or verse in that chapter you want to meditate on.

The more you read a passage or verse over and over again, the easier it is for you to meditate on it.

Use your Bible dictionary to check up

the meanings of difficult words you may

6. Recite the Bible verse over and over

Joshua 1: 8 started by saying, "This book of the law shall not depart out of thy mouth." This verse was not talking about public speaking of the WORD, as in the case of preaching; but own declaration or self-recitation of the commandments, until it becomes implanted in one's memory.

Study has shown that reciting something to oneself improves one's chances of understanding and remembering that thing better. So when you come to a verse you would want to meditate on, recite it to yourself severally. This implants the verse deeper in your memory; but more importantly, the

Holy Spirit quickens your heart with understanding you could never have thought of.

7. Think deep into the passage and relate it to your life

Meditation doesn't end in just reading a verse of the Bible, and memorizing it. That's just the beginning of the process of meditation. You need to look at the passage, verse or the theme over and over again. The reason for this is to understand the word as given by God. As you ponder on the verse or story, ask yourself:

- Who said this?

- Who was it said to?

- Why was it said?

- How does this relate to me?

- What can I do with this?

- Are there other verses that corroborate this one?

As you think about all that, take note of any idea or inspiration that flows into your heart, whether you fully understand it or not.

8. Find a topic and center your meditation around it

Another great way of meditating on the word of God is by centering your meditation on a topic. This is in contrast to picking a verse or passage, reading it and focusing your meditation on it. This method is especially more preferred if there is a theme you are looking to get a grasp of. For example, you are looking at forgiveness or humility; you could look at passages or verses of the Bible that relate to them and use them in meditation.

For instance, looking at Bible for verses surrounding the theme of forgiveness, you can read the following verses:

Mark 11:25 - And when ye stand praying, forgive, if ye have ought against any: that your Father also which is in heaven may forgive you your trespasses.

Ephesians 4:32 - And be ye kind one to another, tenderhearted, forgiving one another, even as God for Christ's sake hath forgiven you.

Matthew 6:15 - But if ye forgive not men their trespasses, neither will your Father forgive your trespasses.

1 John 1:9 - If we confess our sins, he is faithful and just to forgive us [our] sins, and to cleanse us from all unrighteousness.

Matthew 18:21-22 - Then came Peter to him, and said, Lord, how oft shall my brother sin against me, and I forgive him? till seven times? ...

Matthew 6:14-15 - For if ye forgive men their trespasses, your heavenly Father will also forgive you...

James 5:16 - Confess your faults one to another, and pray one for another, that ye may be healed. The effectual fervent prayer of a righteous man availeth much.

Luke 6:27 - But I say unto you which hear, Love your enemies, do good to them which hate you... Judge not, and ye shall not be judged: condemn not, and ye shall not be condemned: forgive, and ye shall be forgiven:

Colossians 3:13 - Forbearing one another, and forgiving one another, if any man have a quarrel against any: even as Christ forgave you, so also do ye.

Psalms 103:10-14 - He hath not dealt with us after our sins; nor rewarded us according to our iniquities...

As you read these scriptures, think on

them, and make notes, you'll find your spirit reaching out to God in prayers.

So, meditating around a subject area instead of a verse, passage or story is also a very great way to enrich your study and meditation time.

9. Listen and hear God speak to you

God is speaking to you in meditation, so listen. You may not feel he's talking to you, but He is.

The Holy Spirit will drop thoughts in your heart while you are meditating. These thoughts will align with God's will and direction for your life. So take note of those thoughts, even if you don't understand them for now. Just write them down. Later on, you'll begin to see how they connect.

The story of Elijah in 1Kings 19 teaches a lot about how God speaks to us. While Elijah was alone on the mountain, there came a furious wind. However, God was not in it. After that, there was an earthquake, then followed by fire, but the Lord was not in any of these. Finally, there was the soft whisper of a voice, and the Lord was in it.

Your period in meditation is when God speaks to you concerning things going on in your life, and those of your family members. He may also speak to you concerning others, and open your eyes and heart to see and accept all He has in store for you.

As far as you learn to open your mind

and listen to God, you will be sure to hear him as he speaks to you

10. Apply the truth you have learnt to your life

Meditation reveals truths to us; application brings about miraculous transformations. When you apply what you learnt during your meditation, you make certain changes to your attitudes that cause supernatural intervention in your life.

God

Bless

You

Other Books from the Same Author

1. <u>Prayer Retreat:</u> 21 Days Devotional With Over 500 Prayers & Declarations to Destroy Stubborn Demonic Problems.

2. <u>HEALING PRAYERS & CONFESSIONS:</u> Daily Meditations, Prayers, and Declarations for Total Healing and Divine Health.

3. <u>200 Violent Prayers</u> for Deliverance, Healing, and Financial Breakthrough.

4. <u>Hearing God's Voice in Painful Moments</u>: Meditations, Prayers, and Declarations to Bring Comfort, Strength, and Healing When Grieving the Loss of Someone You Love.

5 . <u>Healing Prayers:</u> Prophetic Prayers that Brings Healing

6. <u>Healing WORDS:</u> Daily Confessions & Declarations to Activate Your Healing.

7. <u>Prayers That Break Curses</u> and Spells and Release Favors and Breakthroughs.

8. <u>120 Powerful Night Prayers</u> That Will Change Your Life Forever.

9. <u>How to Pray for Your Children Every day:</u> + Prayers & Prophetic Declarations to Use and Pray for Your Children

10. <u>How to Pray for Your Family</u>

11. <u>Daily Prayer Guide:</u> A Practical Guide to Developing a Powerful Personal Prayer Life

12. <u>Make Him Respect You:</u> 31 Very Important Relationship Advice for Women to Make their Men Respect them.

13. <u>How to Cast Out Demons from Your Home, Office & Property:</u> Prayers to Cleanse Your Home, Office, Land & Property from Demonic Attacks

14. <u>Praying Through the Book of Psalms:</u> Selected Psalms, Prayers & Declarations for

Every Situation.

15. <u>STUDENTS' PRAYER BOOK:</u> Motivation & Guide for Students Preparing to Write Exams - Plus 10-Day Prayers for Wisdom, Favor, Protection & Success

16. <u>How to Pray and Receive Financial Miracle</u>: Powerful Prayers for Financial Miracles, Business, and Career Breakthrough

17. <u>Powerful Prayers to Destroy Witchcraft Attacks</u>.

18. <u>Deliverance from Marine Spirits:</u> Prayers to Overcome Marine Spirits – Spirit Husbands and Spirit Wives – Permanently

19. <u>Deliverance From Python Spirit</u>: Prayers to Defeat the Python Spirit – Spirit of Lies, Deceptions, and Oppression.

20. <u>Anger Management God's Way</u>: Controlling Your Emotions, Getting Healed of Hurts & Responding to Offenses ...Plus: Daily Prayers to Overcome Bad Anger Permanently

21. <u>How God Speaks to You</u>: Simple Guide to Hearing the Voice of God Clearly & Following His Direction for Your Life

22. <u>Deliverance of the Mind</u>: Prayers to Deal With Mind Control, Fear, Anxiety, Depression, Anger and Other Negative Emotions

23. <u>Most Commonly Asked Questions About Demons:</u> How to Cast Out Demons and, Obtain Deliverance.

24. <u>Praying the Promises of God</u> for Daily Blessings and Breakthrough.

25. <u>When God Is Silent</u>! What to Do When Prayer Seems Unanswered or Delayed

26. <u>I SHALL NOT DIE</u>: Prayers to Overcome the Spirit and Fear of Death.

27. <u>Praise Warfare:</u> Overcoming Your Fears, Worries & Battles With Praise

Get in Touch

We love testimonies. We love to hear what God is doing around the world as people draw close to Him in prayer. Please share your story with us.

Also, please consider giving this book a review on Amazon and checking out our other titles at www.amazon.com/author/danielokpara .

I also invite you to check out our website at www.BetterLifeWorld.org and consider joining our newsletter, which we send out once in a while with great tips, testimonies, and revelations from God's Word for victorious living.

Feel free to drop us your prayer request. We will join faith with you, and God's power will be released in your life and the issue in question.

About the Author.

Daniel Chika Okpara is a husband, father, pastor, businessman and lecturer. He has authored over 50 life-transforming books on business, prayer, relationship and victorious living.

He is the president of Better Life World Outreach Centre -www.betterlifeworld.org - a non-denominational evangelism ministry committed to global prayer revival, empowerment and evangelism.

Through the monthly Better Life Crusades, Breakthrough Seminars, and Better Life TV, thousands of lives are coming to the LORD, healed, blessed and restored to a purposeful living.

He holds a Master's Degree in Theology from Cornerstone Christian University and is married to Prophetess Doris Okpara, his prayer warrior, best friend and biggest support in life. They are blessed with two lovely children.

NOTES